Key Battles of World War I

David Taylor

H www.heinemann.co.uk
Visit our website to find out more information about Heinemann Library books.

To order:
☎ Phone 44 (0) 1865 888066
🖷 Send a fax to 44 (0) 1865 314091
💻 Visit the Heinemann Bookshop at www.heinemann.co.uk to browse our catalogue and order online.

First published in Great Britain by Heinemann Library,
Halley Court, Jordan Hill, Oxford OX2 8EJ,
a division of Reed Educational and Professional Publishing Ltd.
Heinemann is a registered trademark of Reed Educational and Professional Publishing Ltd.

OXFORD MELBOURNE AUCKLAND
JOHANNESBURG BLANTYRE GABORONE
IBADAN PORTSMOUTH (NH) USA CHICAGO

Designed by AMR
Illustrated by Art Construction and David Cuzik
Originated by Dot Gradations
Printed by Wing King Tong in Hong Kong.

ISBN 0 431 11981 3 (hardback)   ISBN 0 431 11988 0 (paperback)
06 05 04 03 02   06 05 04 03 02
10 9 8 7 6 5 4 3 2   10 9 8 7 6 5 4 3 2 1

British Library Cataloguing in Publication Data
Taylor, David, 1945 –
Key battles of World War One. – (20th century perspectives)
1. World War, 1914–1918 – Campaigns – Juvenile literature
I.Title
940.4

Acknowledgements
The publishers would like to thank the following for permission to reproduce photographs:
Corbis, pp.24, 25, 40, 43; Hulton Getty, pp.23, 27, 37; Imperial War Museum, pp.10, 11, 13, 15, 16, 17, 19, 20, 21, 29, 31, 32, 34, 39; John Frost, p. 42; Peter Newark, p.18; The Art Archive, pp. 5, 36; unknown, p.41.

Cover photograph reproduced with permission of Corbis.

Every effort has been made to contact copyright holders of any material reproduced in this book. Any omissions will be rectified in subsequent printings if notice is given to the publishers.

Words appearing in the text in bold, **like this**, are explained in the glossary.

Contents

War clouds gather

Before 1914, there was great rivalry between the **great powers** of Europe. This rivalry resulted in the outbreak of World War One in August 1914. People thought that 'it would be all over by Christmas'. How wrong they were! The war lasted for four long years. More than eight million soldiers were killed and over twenty million more were wounded and disabled. So just what were the rivalries that brought about this terrible war?

France and Germany

In 1870–1, Germany defeated France in the Franco-Prussian War. The Germans took over the French provinces of Alsace and Lorraine. The French wanted their land back and thirsted for revenge.

Britain and Germany

Germany had grown into a powerful country with a large army. It was also busy building up its navy and winning an overseas **empire**. All of this worried the British. Britain had the largest empire in the world and its navy had ruled the oceans for a hundred years. It did not like being challenged by Germany. The two countries became jealous of each other.

This map shows Europe in January 1914.

Key
Triple Entente (The Allies)
Triple Alliance (Central Powers)
Turkey joined the Central Powers in October 1914. Italy joined the Allies in 1915.

Russia and Austria-Hungary

Austria-Hungary had a large empire in central Europe. It wanted to take over land in an area in south-east Europe known as the **Balkans**. In 1908, Austria-Hungary took control of the small Balkan country of Bosnia. The biggest Balkan country, Serbia, did not like this and wanted to drive the Austrians out. Russia was also interested in the Balkans. It wanted to have access from the Black Sea to the Mediterranean Sea through the Straits of Dardanelles. Russia supported Serbia against the Austrians, but the Austrians had the backing of Germany. It was a tense situation.

The alliance system

The mistrust and suspicion between the great powers led them to group themselves into two **alliances**. Germany, Austria-Hungary and Italy formed the Triple Alliance. This was rivalled by the Triple Entente (*entente* is French for 'agreement'), made up of Britain, France and Russia. If two countries from the rival alliances went to war, the other four countries would be involved in one way or another. Europe was living on a knife-edge.

A fateful day

On 28 June 1914, Archduke Franz Ferdinand, the heir to the Austrian throne, and his wife Sophie, paid a state visit to Sarajevo, the capital city of Bosnia. While driving through the streets in an open-top car, the archduke and his wife were shot dead by Gavrilo Princip, a young Serbian student. The Austrians blamed Serbia for the shootings and this set off a chain reaction of events that, by early August, had plunged Europe into World War One.

A costly wrong turning

The chauffeur of Archduke Franz Ferdinand's car was named Leopold Lojka. As he drove from Sarajevo station to the town hall, Lojka noticed a member of the crowd about to throw a grenade at the car. He immediately accelerated, causing the **grenade** to land on the rolled-up hood of the car, rather than inside it. The grenade fell to the ground. Lojka's quick thinking saved the life of the Archduke, who was left shocked and angry.

When they reached the town hall, the archduke decided to leave Sarajevo as quickly as possible. A new route was drawn up back to the station, but no one told Lojka! As the procession of cars drove off, Lojka turned right off Franz Joseph Avenue instead of going straight on. He went to turn round, but could not find reverse gear. Princip seized the moment, ran from the crowd and shot the archduke in the jugular vein. Sophie, who was pregnant, was shot in the stomach.

The Battle of the Marne 1914

The outbreak of war was greeted with joy and enthusiasm by many people on all sides. From all over the British **Empire** men volunteered to fight. They came from Australia, New Zealand, South Africa, Canada, India and the West Indies. It was thought that the war would be over by the end of the year, but it continued until 1918, mainly because the Germans lost the Battle of the Marne.

The Schlieffen Plan

A German general, Count Alfred von Schlieffen, had made up a plan to knock France out of the war within six weeks. This was to avoid having to fight a war on two fronts. German troops would march through Belgium into northern France and encircle Paris. Once France was beaten, German troops would be sent to fight Russia in eastern Europe.

To begin with, things went well for the Germans. Powerful guns destroyed Belgian forts and allowed the German **infantry** and **cavalry** to advance rapidly. The Belgians fought heroically, but were no match for the might of the German army.

On 22 August 1914, the British Expeditionary Force (BEF), an army of 100,000 men, arrived at Mons in Belgium. Here, the BEF managed to delay the German army, but was then forced to retreat.

The Schlieffen Plan and the Battle of the Marne 1914.

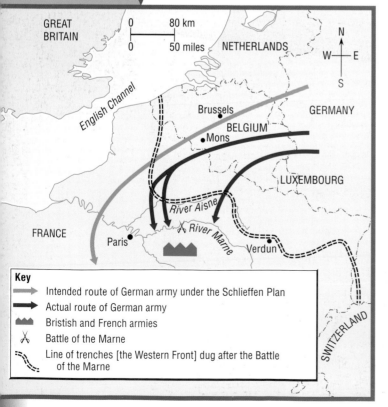

The Battle of the Marne, 5–9 September 1914

The German army had been covering up to 50 kilometres a day and was becoming tired. It had also lost around 100,000 men, who had been sent to fight the Russians on the Eastern Front. So, General von Kluck decided to change the Schlieffen Plan. Instead of sweeping westwards around Paris, he ordered the German army to swing to the east.

The British and French gathered their forces together along the River Marne, and decided to make a stand against the Germans. Over 4000 French reinforcements were rushed to the battlefield by taxi from Paris! The battle lasted for five days and ended with the exhausted Germans being pushed back 60 kilometres to the River Aisne. The **Allies** called their victory 'the miracle of the Marne'. Paris had been saved from capture, and German hopes of beating France quickly lay in ruins.

British troops come under fire during the Battle of the Marne. One soldier has been shot, and another soldier runs for cover.

Stalemate

The Battle of the Marne was a turning-point. Up to now the war had been one of movement. But both sides realized that their modern guns were so accurate and powerful, they would have to dig in and fight a defensive war. It was impossible for infantry and cavalry to move across the open countryside without being shot down. Both sides dug a line of trenches from the English Channel to the Swiss border – the **Western Front**. The war had reached a stalemate.

War breaks out – how did people react?

The atmosphere was electric, almost unbelievable. We were all excited about it and ready to join in.

Norman Tennant of the British Royal Field Artillery

In Australia at that time we were part of the British Empire and very loyal to Britain. We thought it was our war.

Edward Smout, Australian Medical Corps

We believed that the French army would perform miracles. We did not think for one moment that the war would go on so long or would be so cruel.

Hermine Venot-Focke, French civilian, 1914

Everyone was waving flags. We threw flowers to the marching soldiers. Everyone was singing, 'We'll meet again in the Fatherland'.

Margarethe Stahl, German civilian, 1914

Trench systems and warfare

The trench systems built along the **Western Front** were very complicated. The British front-line trenches were between two and three metres deep and 1.5 metre wide. Either wood or corrugated iron strengthened the sides. Huge rolls of barbed wire up to 30 metres wide protected them. Behind the front-line trench were support trenches and communication trenches, along which supplies and troops were moved. The support trenches had **latrines**, kitchens and stores. Behind the trench system were artillery posts, ammunition dumps and field hospitals.

The German trenches were much deeper than the British ones. Some of them were as deep as 15 metres, with underground sick bays and sleeping quarters for the troops. They often had electric lights, piped water and good ventilation.

The area between the two lines of trenches was known as **No Man's Land**. It was usually about 500 metres wide, but sometimes was as narrow as 50 metres.

This diagram shows a typical trench system on the Western Front.

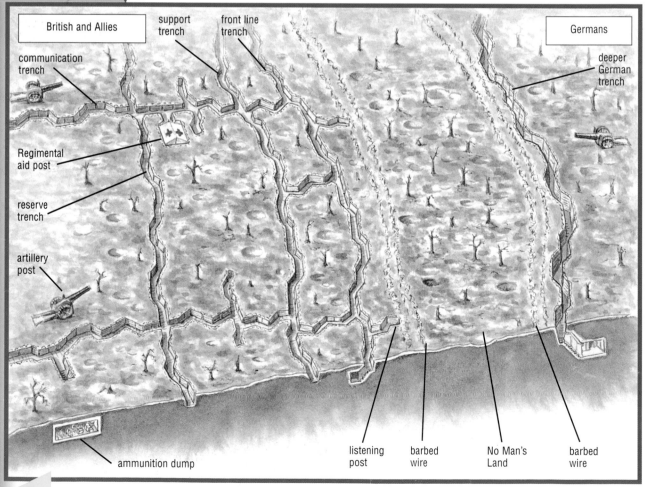

British and Allies | Germans

communication trench · support trench · front line trench · deeper German trench · Regimental aid post · reserve trench · artillery post · ammunition dump · listening post · barbed wire · No Man's Land · barbed wire

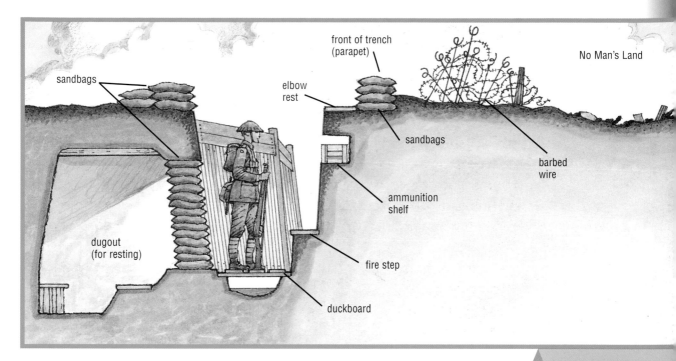

Labels on diagram:
sandbags
dugout (for resting)
elbow rest
front of trench (parapet)
sandbags
No Man's Land
barbed wire
ammunition shelf
fire step
duckboard

Trench warfare

A major attack on the enemy lines began with an artillery barrage that usually lasted for days. The idea was to unnerve the enemy and destroy the barbed wire in front of their trenches. Often, however, the shells were duds or fell short and only succeeded in churning up No Man's Land. Sometimes the enemy withdrew from the front-line trench and returned once the gunfire had stopped. After the bombardment, soldiers fixed **bayonets** on to their rifles and went 'over the top' of the trench into No Man's Land to attack the enemy trenches. They usually walked straight into a hail of machine-gun fire and were mown down in their hundreds. Casualties were very high and gains of land were minimal.

Stretcher-bearers fetched wounded soldiers from No Man's Land. They took them to the Regimental Aid Post, where they were given first aid. Then, they were taken to the **casualty clearing station** behind the lines, where they were operated on if their injuries were serious.

A cross-section through a British front-line trench on the Western Front. Sandbags protected the soldiers from enemy fire.

Eyewitnesses

In the daytime you couldn't put your finger above the parapet, let alone your head (for fear of enemy snipers). One young chap jumped on the fire step and looked out across No Man's Land. He was hit in the forehead and was dead before he'd been there three minutes.

Harry Smith, of the British Royal Norfolk Regiment

Brought the wounded down from the front line today. Conditions terrible. The ground is a quagmire. It needs six men to carry each stretcher. The mud was sometimes up to our waists.

From the diary of Sergeant Robert McKay, a British stretcher-bearer in World War One.

Life in the trenches

Life in the front-line trenches was gruesome. Soldiers usually spent sixteen days on trench duty: eight in the front-line trenches, four in reserve and four in the rest camp. Even when they were not under attack, the men had a lot to put up with and had to be tough to survive the dreadful conditions.

Conditions in the trenches

In the summer the trenches were very hot and dusty. But the winters were worse. Heavy rain caused the trenches to flood and men often had to stand knee deep in liquid mud. In frosty weather the duckboards (paths built of wooden slats that ran along the trenches) would freeze over, making it difficult to stand up. Many of the **Empire** soldiers had never seen snow or felt so cold, and were issued with woollen underpants. Many men suffered from trenchfoot, when feet swelled up due to standing in water for long periods. It was so painful it made men scream and cry.

Many soldiers suffered from shell-shock, a kind of nervous breakdown brought on by fear, stress and the miserable conditions. Some soldiers were unable to utter a word; others trembled and shook.

It was impossible to get a proper wash, so skin diseases were common. Soldiers' clothes became impregnated with body lice, causing the skin to itch. Men would remove their jackets and run a lit cigarette down the seams in order to burn the eggs of the lice. This gave some relief, but the lice soon returned. The lice also caused trench fever, a kind of flu.

British soldiers using a pump to drain a front-line trench in January 1917.

A lasting stench

The familiar trench smell still haunts my nostrils. Made up of stagnant mud, latrine buckets, chloride of lime, unburied bodies, rotting sandbags, stale human sweat and fumes of cordite.

A World War One soldier remembers the smell of the trenches years later.

The trenches were infested with rats, some as large as small cats. They fed off scraps of food and the rotting flesh of dead bodies. The men hated the rats almost as much as the shelling.

The food was not very appetizing. Men lived on tinned corned beef ('bully beef'), biscuits, bread and cheese. They were also given tins of Maconochie, a stew which they ate either hot or cold. Sometimes they had bacon and Tommy Tickler's jam (tinned jam made of plums and apples). The drinking water was supplied in petrol cans and was chlorinated to kill the germs. Not surprisingly, it tasted awful.

An Australian soldier using a periscope to look out over No Man's Land. His colleagues are manning the fire step.

Daily routine in the trenches

Life in the **Allied** front line began at dawn with the 'daily hate': giving the enemy a volley of rifle and machine-gun fire. The men then had to clean their guns ready for inspection. After breakfast there were a variety of jobs to be done. Duckboards had to be repaired or replaced, and sandbags filled. The rest of the day was spent playing cards, reading, writing letters home and trying to get some much-needed sleep in one of the dugouts. At dusk, food supplies and water were carried up to the front along the communication trenches. At any one time, about a third of the men were on sentry duty. This was hard work, as it was necessary to concentrate for two hours at a time.

There was a lot of activity at night. Some repaired the barbed wire. Others raided the enemy trenches. Parties of men crawled over **No Man's Land** and threw **grenades** into the enemy trench. At other times, soldiers crouched in listening posts trying to find out what the enemy was doing.

The relief of trench units also took place at night. The new soldiers had to wade through the wet, winding communication trenches laden down with rolls of barbed wire, shovels, picks and corrugated iron. The soldiers going off trench duty could look forward to a hot bath, a proper meal and some leisure time in the local town.

The Battle of the Somme 1916

The Battle of the Somme, 1 July to 18 November 1916.

In 1916 the British and French launched an attack on the German lines along the River Somme in northern France. The British commander, Sir Douglas Haig, aimed to push back the Germans and kill as many enemy soldiers as possible. He believed that a breakthrough could be made in a matter of hours. The attack was also designed to take the pressure off the French, who from February 1916 were desperately defending Verdun, a fortress town in Eastern France, from a huge German onslaught.

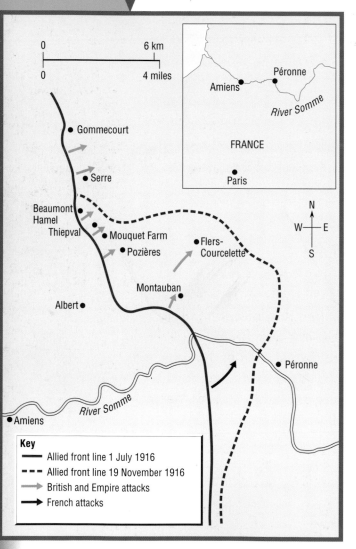

Key
— Allied front line 1 July 1916
--- Allied front line 19 November 1916
→ British and Empire attacks
→ French attacks

CASUALTIES ON THE SOMME	
BRITAIN AND EMPIRE	420,000
FRANCE	200,000
GERMANY	450,000

Bombardment

On 24 June 1916, over 1500 **Allied** guns began to bombard the German trenches. The barrage went on for seven days. The intention was to 'soften up' the Germans and to destroy their trenches and the barbed wire that protected them. In fact, the guns were not powerful enough and many shells landed short of their target, leaving huge craters in **No Man's Land**. It would be difficult for any army to cross.

A day of carnage

On the morning of 1 July 1916, the guns fell silent. It was a fine morning and the birds could be heard singing. At 7.30 a.m., 'zero hour', waves of British soldiers were sent over the top. They were told that the artillery bombardment would have destroyed the enemy trenches and they were to walk in straight lines across No Man's Land. It sounded easy.

However, the barbed wire was still in place and the German trenches still intact. They were much deeper than the British trenches and the German soldiers had been well sheltered. They emerged from their shelters and manned their machine guns. The advancing British troops were mown down 'like swathes of cut corn at harvest time'. It was utter carnage. In an attack on Serre, the

Accrington **pals battalion** lost 584 men out of 720. Near Beaumont Hamel, the Newfoundland Regiment lost 684 men out of 752. At the end of the day the British casualties stood at 57,470, of which 19,240 were dead. It remains the worst day in British military history.

The campaign continues

In Britain, the newspapers reported on a successful day! Then the full horror of what had happened began to sink in. Haig, however, still believed he could wear down the Germans, and he ordered further attacks over the next five months.

On 15 September, the British used tanks for the first time, in an attack at Flers-Courcelette. They were not very successful. Only 49 were available to Haig and most of them kept breaking down.

As winter approached, rain set in and the trenches became very muddy. On 18 November, Haig called off the Somme campaign. The Allies had gained a mere 15 kilometres of ground at a massive cost. Haig was criticized for sending so many men to their deaths. But later the Germans said that the battle had taken so much out of their army that it helped towards their eventual defeat in 1918.

A wave of British troops walk across No Man's Land on 1 July 1916. Another group of soldiers can just be seen waiting in the trenches for their turn to go 'over the top'.

A book that stopped a bullet

*We went into the ruined village of Montauban. As we turned a corner there was a German machine-gunner waiting for us. He got me in the foot and I felt two kicks over my heart. I went at him and **bayonetted** him. I sat down to see what the damage was. My foot was bad, but when I looked at my left-hand breast pocket I saw two holes in it. I opened my pocket and found two bullets had gone through my metal shaving mirror and had nosed their way into a book I was carrying. Funnily enough, earlier in the morning my officer had given me the book and said I could read it when I got into the German trenches. So I put it in my pocket, little thinking that I should be able to read it on a hospital ship coming home.*

A British sergeant describes his lucky escape in the *Manchester Guardian*, 8 July 1916.

The Third Battle of Ypres 1917

The Third Battle of Ypres, also known as the Battle of Passchendaele, was fought between 31 July and 10 November 1917.

The plan

In May 1917, **Sir Douglas Haig** made plans for an all-out **offensive** against the German line near Ypres in the low-lying area of Flanders, a part of Belgium. He believed that the German army was weakening and now was the time to 'break its heart'. If the **Allies** could break through the German lines into open country, the way was open to attack the German-occupied ports of Ostend and Zeebrugge, which were key **U-boat** bases. After that the Allies would advance on Germany itself.

On 7 June, as a prelude to the battle, the Allies captured the Messines Ridge to the south of Ypres. The attack was then called off. The British prime minister, David Lloyd George, was worried that too many soldiers would be killed. Haig persuaded the prime minister that the attack was needed if Britain was to win the war. He won the argument, and in July was allowed to resume the campaign. The lull had given the Germans time to fortify their trenches with concrete **pillboxes** and prepare for the attack.

At the Third Battle of Ypres, in 1917, the Allies hoped to break through the German lines and capture Ostend and Zeebrugge. Ypres is about 60 km from Ostend.

The battle begins

On 16 July, the Allies began a fifteen-day artillery barrage against the German trenches at Pilckem, to the north of Ypres. Over four million shells were fired. As well as damaging the German trenches, the shells also destroyed the drains and dykes that drained the area of water. At 3.50 a.m. on 31 July, General Hubert Gough's men were sent over the top. The weather was atrocious. It was pouring with rain and the battlefield was like 'muddy porridge'. The British expected to gain over 4000 metres of ground on the first day, but they were pushed back by the Germans, losing 27,000 men in the process.

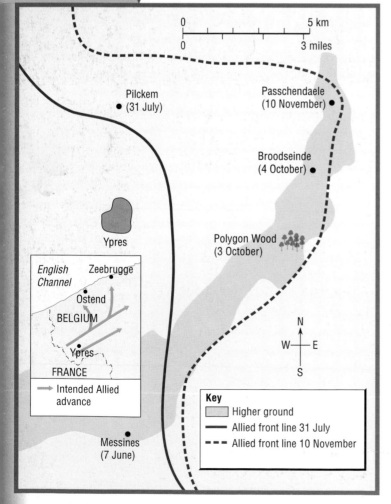

0 ____ 5 km
0 ____ 3 miles

Pilckem (31 July)

Passchendaele (10 November)

Broodseinde (4 October)

Polygon Wood (3 October)

Ypres

English Channel — Zeebrugge — Ostend — BELGIUM — Ypres — FRANCE

→ Intended Allied advance

N / W—E / S

Messines (7 June)

Key
- Higher ground
- Allied front line 31 July
- - - Allied front line 10 November

> ## Drowning in the mud
>
> *From the darkness and on all sides came the groans and wails of wounded men; faint, long, sobbing moans of agony, and despairing shrieks. It was too horribly obvious that dozens of men with serious wounds must have crawled for safety into new shell holes, and now the water was rising about them and, powerless to move, they were slowly drowning.*
>
> From the diary of Edward Campion Vaughan, a British officer, 27 August 1917

A sea of mud

August was very wet. With no drainage the whole area around Ypres became a sea of mud. Still the British continued to attack. By 25 September, five kilometres of ground had been won at a cost of 86,000 casualties. The rain continued. Tanks became stuck in the mud and supplies had to be carried up to the front over slippery planks of wood.

Stretcher-bearers, knee deep in mud, struggle to rescue a wounded man from No Man's Land during the Third Battle of Ypres, 1917.

Stretcher-bearers were hampered by the thick mud in **No Man's Land**. Hundreds of wounded soldiers were drowned before help could get to them. In early October the weather improved and British and **ANZAC** troops gained territory at Polygon Wood and Broodseinde.

Passchendaele falls

In late October, Canadian troops launched an attack on the village of Passchendaele, which was situated on a ridge of higher ground. If this ridge was captured, the Allies would have a dry spot to spend the winter. At 6.00 a.m. on 6 November, the Canadians went 'over the top'. The fighting was fierce but they managed to capture the now ruined village. On 10 November, the Allied forces called off the campaign.

Altogether, eight kilometres of ground had been gained in three and a half months of fighting. Haig's aim of breaking through the German lines and into open country had not been achieved. The Allies and the Germans had both lost about 300,000 men. The Germans had lost some of their best soldiers, and morale was now very low in their army.

Technology and new weapons

World War One was fought between **industrialized** countries that had scientists and engineers capable of making weapons of mass destruction. During the war, two new weapons were produced which were meant to break the deadlock of trench warfare. They had mixed success.

Tanks

In 1912 an Australian, L. E. Moles, suggested building an armour-plated, bullet-proof vehicle with guns that could be used to bulldoze through enemy lines. He was ignored! When World War One broke out, a British soldier, Colonel Ernest Swinton, persuaded Winston Churchill, the First Lord of the Admiralty, to look at the idea again. Swinton argued that an armoured vehicle with caterpillar tracks would be able to travel over rough ground and smash through barbed wire and trenches. It could also knock out the enemy's machine guns, allowing the **infantry** to move in.

In 1915 a model tank called *Little Willie* was built, and from this the first really practicable *Mark I* tank was developed. In February 1916 the *Mark I* was demonstrated to **Lord Kitchener**, the Minister for War, in Hatfield Park, north of London. He was not impressed and said it would never win the war. However, **Sir Douglas Haig** thought it was worth trying and, in September 1916, 49 tanks were used in the Battle of the Somme. Unfortunately, they were very slow, kept breaking down and clearly had teething problems. Haig still thought they had potential and asked the British government to supply the army with 1000 more tanks.

A British tank in action at Thiepval during the Battle of the Somme on 25 September, 1916.

In 1917 the faster *Whippet* tank was built and successfully used in the Battle of Cambrai, the first time that tanks were used *en masse*. In 1918 the British and Americans jointly produced the *Mark VIII* (or *Liberty*) tank. It weighed 37 tonnes, carried a crew of eight and could fire 208 shells and 13,000 bullets. The main difference between it and earlier tanks was that the engine was separated from the crew's compartment. Although not yet perfect, the tank had shown itself to be a weapon for the future.

Poisonous gases

Chlorine gas was first used by the Germans in April 1915. Containers of gas were opened and it was allowed to drift towards the enemy. The problem for the attacking side was that if the wind changed direction the gas could be blown back towards them. Gas was meant to disrupt the enemy before an attack was made, and it succeeded. The first gas attacks caused panic among the troops. They had never experienced anything like it before. Chlorine gas filled the lungs with fluid, and this often resulted in death from suffocation.

World War One troops suffering from the effects of mustard gas, in a painting by the American artist, John Singer Sargent.

The British soon developed their own chlorine gas, which they used against the Germans in the Battle of Loos in September 1915. By 1917, the Germans were using mustard gas. This was much more lethal, causing sickness, internal bleeding, blindness and burning of the skin. By now gas was fired in shells from long-range guns, so it did not matter from which direction the wind was blowing.

Initially, soldiers protected themselves from gas by wearing goggles and putting handkerchiefs soaked in urine over their mouths. Later, face masks with air tubes and filters were introduced and, although they gave better protection, they made it difficult for the soldiers to breathe and move. During the war over 91,000 soldiers were killed by gas and a further 1,200,000 were injured by it.

GAS PRODUCTION IN WORLD WAR ONE

GERMANY	69,000 TONNES
FRANCE	38,000 TONNES
BRITAIN	25,000 TONNES

Not a joy ride!

Tanks were terribly noisy, oily, hot, airless and bumpy! As they had no springs and weighed 30 tonnes, any slight bump was magnified, throwing the crew about. If the tank was hit in action, pieces of hot steel flew around. Bullets hitting the armoured plates caused the steel to melt and splash. It was dangerous to the eyes.

A British tank commander describing what it was like inside a World War One tank.

The Battle of Cambrai 1917

In August 1917, Colonel John Fuller of the British Tank Corps suggested a massed tank attack on the German lines to the south-west of Cambrai in northern France. The land here was made up of gentle chalk hills and was well drained and dry. It was ideal terrain for tanks. After some discussion, Sir Douglas Haig, Commander-in-Chief of the British army, agreed, and planning for the Battle of Cambrai began in earnest.

The plan

The attack on the German lines would be made up of four phases.

1 An advance line of tanks would move into **No Man's Land** and crush the barbed wire protecting the German trenches.
2 The main group of tanks would follow and cross the German trenches by dropping their **fascines** into them.
3 The **infantry** would then move in and clear the German trenches of any enemy soldiers.
4 The **cavalry** would burst through the gaps made in the trenches and surround the town of Cambrai.

Preparations

The date for the attack was to be 20 November 1917. For two weeks before the attack, the British soldiers underwent detailed training. The Tank Corps was anxious to succeed. So far, the performance of the tank in battle had been disappointing and many generals did not think it was much help. Tanks were transported to the battlefield at night by railway and hidden from the view of the Germans. It was decided not to have the usual preliminary artillery barrage, as this would warn the Germans that an attack was imminent.

A painting by W. L. Wyllie showing British tanks rolling into action at Cambrai.

The battle

At 6.20 a.m. over 1000 British guns started to bombard the German trenches and immediately the first of 378 British tanks rumbled into No Man's Land. They were supported by 289 aircraft, which attacked enemy gun batteries. The tanks moved forward, crushing barbed wire and using their fascines to cross over the German trenches. The Germans had been taken completely by surprise and they were powerless to stop the advance. At the end of the day six kilometres of territory had been gained over a ten-kilometre front. The supporting infantry had taken 6000 prisoners. When news of this success reached England, church bells were rung in celebration.

British tanks moving forward during the Battle of Cambrai. The dry ground was ideally suited for a tank attack.

It was not a complete success, as 179 tanks had been lost either to enemy gunfire or because of mechanical breakdown. Some got stuck trying to cross the trenches. By 23 November, only 92 tanks were working and there were none in reserve to keep up the pressure. When the cavalry moved in they were driven back by German gunfire. There was also not enough infantry in reserve.

The Germans moved reinforcements into the area, and on 30 November launched a fierce counter-attack, using artillery, aircraft and gas. They managed to win back nearly all of the ground they had lost. At the end of the fighting both sides had lost about 45,000 men. Although it was not a decisive victory, the tanks had proved their worth and shown they were a weapon of the future. For the tank, the Battle of Cambrai was a turning-point.

Tanks go into battle

My tank was in the second wave of attack. At 6.30 a.m., I gave the 'right away' and our engine purred with perfect tuning. As the mist cleared I found it possible to recognize all the features shown on the air photos and maps, and the going was easy over the rolling grassy slopes. Our infantry waved us on. The enemy fire withered and it became clear that the fantastic sight of all our monsters approaching had demoralized the Germans. Our infantry had little to do but to receive the prisoners and clear the dug-outs in the trenches.

Lieutenant Gordon Hassell, of the Tank Corps, describes the first day of the Battle of Cambrai.

Women on the Western Front

Women were not allowed to fight but this did not prevent them from going to the **Western Front** to provide vital support for the soldiers. Women from all the **Allied** countries were keen to show their patriotism and to prove they were the equals of men. As well as on the Western Front, women also served on the **Eastern Front**, in Gallipoli and the Middle East.

A 1915 recruiting poster for the Voluntary Aid Detachment.

Women's organizations

The First Aid Nursing Yeomanry (FANYs) enlisted women to support the troops in Belgium and France. They helped out as nurses in field hospitals, drove ambulances and set up troops canteens. The Voluntary Aid Detachment (VADs) sent over 8000 women to northern France to work as nurses, mechanics, ambulance drivers, clerical workers, cleaners and cooks. To begin with, VADs were looked down upon by the soldiers and nicknamed 'Very Active Dusters'! But very soon, as with all women at the front, they won respect and admiration for the work they did.

Over 16,000 American women flocked to Europe to help the Allied war effort. They worked as nurses, secretaries, welfare workers and canteen workers. In 1918 over 200 highly trained American women served

Sister Pearl Corkhill

Pearl Corkhill was an Australian nurse working close to the front line in a **casualty clearing station**. In July 1918, German aircraft twice bombed the clearing station. Pearl was awarded the Military Medal for her bravery. She wrote to her mother to tell her the news:

Today word came that I had been awarded the Military Medal. Well the Commanding Officer sent over a bottle of champagne and they all drank my health and now the medical officers are giving me a dinner in honour of the event. I can't see what I've done to deserve it but the part I don't like is having to face old George and Mary [the king and queen] to get the medal. It will cost me a new mess dress, but I suppose I should not grumble at that – I'm still wearing the one I left Australia in.

with the US Signal Corps. Nicknamed 'hello girls', they worked as telephone operators in France. The Australian Army Nursing Service sent over 2000 nurses to Europe to serve in military hospitals.

Hardship and danger

Women support workers at the front had to put up with the same conditions

Canadian nurses clearing up after a bomb had hit their living quarters. Two nurses were killed in this attack at Étaples in France.

as the soldiers. They lived in huts and tents with few comforts. Getting a proper wash was almost impossible. Women were also in danger of being gassed or shelled. In 1917 a military hospital run by American nurses was bombed, causing the deaths of several patients and injuring nurses. Elsie Grey, a New Zealand nurse, described in her diary how a shell hit the tents they were living in: 'The shell burst and a piece of shrapnel shot through the tent piercing an artery of a British nurse. Ten minutes later she was dead.' One VAD grew so distressed at the number of wounded soldiers she saw that she jumped off a cliff and killed herself. Disease and illness were also a problem. Many women suffered from exhaustion, lice, shell-shock and influenza.

The Madonnas of Pervyse

In 1914 two British women, Mairi Chisholm and Elsie Knocker, went to Belgium to work as ambulance drivers. Together they set up a first-aid station very close to the front line at Pervyse. They went into **No Man's Land**, often under fire, to bring back wounded soldiers. They treated the soldiers at their first-aid post before sending them on to a military hospital. Soldiers looked after by Mairi and Elsie knew they were in good hands and nicknamed them 'the two Madonnas of Pervyse'. In March 1918,22 both women were gassed during a German attack. Only then did they return to Britain after four years of heroic work.

The Gallipoli Campaign 1915

In October 1914, Turkey entered the war on the side of Germany. By early 1915, there was a stalemate on the **Western Front**, so the British government decided to attack Turkey. If Turkey was forced out of the war, the **Allies** could attack Austria-Hungary from the south and send supplies through the Black Sea to Russia. (See map on page 4.)

The plan was to send a fleet of ships to force its way through the Straits of Dardanelles, a narrow stretch of water that leads into the Black Sea. Once through the Straits, the ships would advance on Constantinople and make Turkey surrender. The Straits were guarded on either side by Turkish forts and guns. The British believed that the Turks would not fight very hard and that their guns were out of date. In February and March 1915, British and French ships bombarded the Turkish forts and tried to sail through the Straits. They were forced back by gunfire and **minefields**. Three ships were sunk by mines, and three were badly damaged, with a loss of 700 men.

The Gallipoli Campaign in Turkey lasted for eight months in 1915. Despite the bravery of the Allied troops the campaign ended in failure.

25 April 1915 – a day to forget

A change of plan was called for. It was decided to land troops on the Gallipoli peninsula and capture the Turkish forts. Then the ships would be able to sail through the Straits unopposed. On 25 April 1915, a force of British, French, Indian and **ANZAC** soldiers, commanded by General Sir Ian Hamilton, landed on the narrow beaches of Gallipoli.

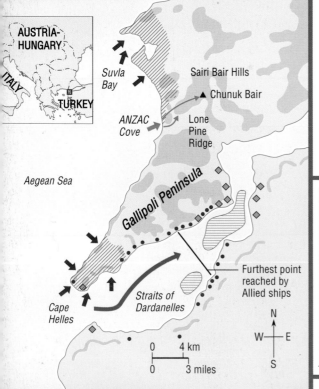

Unfortunately, the British commanders had not done enough planning. The troops were short of guns and there were no specialist landing craft. Instead, the troops were put ashore in rowing boats. There were no engineers and equipment to build jetties, so that supplies could be landed quickly. The officers in charge did not account for the steep cliffs that rose up from some of the beaches. The Turks had positioned machine-gun units on the top of the cliffs. As the Allied troops clambered up the cliffs, they came under heavy fire and suffered terrible casualties.

Key
- Highland
- Turkish minefields
- ◇ Turkish forts
- • Smaller Turkish guns
- ➡ Naval advance Feb/March
- ➡ British landings 25 April
- ➡ ANZAC landings 25 April
- ➡ British landings 6 August
- → ANZAC attacks 6 August
- Ground gained by Allies

The fiasco continues

The Allies advanced just five kilometres, before digging themselves into trenches. It was stalemate again, just like the Western Front. Dead bodies lay everywhere. The smell of rotting flesh was so strong that a truce was called so that the dead could be buried. The hot summer sun beat down on the Allied soldiers. Water was in short supply, and flies and lice were everywhere. Soon, 200 men a day were falling sick with dysentery, fever and typhoid.

On 6 August, Allied reinforcements landed at Suvla Bay. They fought bravely but, once again, the determined Turks beat them off and stopped them from advancing inland. The Allies were again forced to dig trenches to defend themselves. By November winter had set in and soldiers began to die of frostbite. It was clear that the invasion of Gallipoli had failed. In December the disastrous campaign was called off. By 9 January 1916, the surviving 135,000 Allied troops had been evacuated in a brilliant operation – the only success of a disastrous campaign. The Allies had lost 265,000 men, including 36,000 ANZAC troops.

Terrible injuries

Men had lost arms and legs, brains oozed out of skulls, and lungs protruded from riven chests; many had lost their faces. One poor chap had lost his nose and we also had to take off an arm, a hand and extract two bullets like shark's teeth from his thigh. I saw him the next morning being carried to the mortuary.

A medical orderly describes the injuries received by the Allied forces on 25 April 1915.

ANZAC troops landing at the Cove named after them, on 25 April 1915. The steep cliffs overlooking the narrow beach are clearly visible.

The ANZACS

'ANZAC' was short for the 'Australian and New Zealand Army Corps'. The Australian troops were nicknamed 'diggers' and were famous for their courage and cheerfulness during the heat of battle. In Australia and New Zealand, the heroism and sacrifices of the troops at Gallipoli are remembered each year on 25 April – ANZAC Day.

The landings at Suvla Bay 1915

In the summer of 1915, the fighting in Gallipoli was deadlocked. Both sides had dug trenches and were defending their positions. In August Sir Ian Hamilton decided to attack the Turks again in an effort to win control of the Gallipoli peninsula. It was to be a two-pronged attack. Australian and New Zealand troops were to break out of their base at **ANZAC** Cove and attack the Turkish guns in the Sairi Bair hills. Eight kilometres further north fresh British troops were to be landed on the poorly defended beaches of Suvla Bay. (See map on page 22.)

The Australians at Lone Pine Ridge

On the afternoon of 6 August 1915, the Australians, under **General Sir William Birdwood**, attacked the Turkish trenches at Lone Pine Ridge. They were inexperienced soldiers but fought with great courage. The fighting was hand to hand, with rifles and **bayonets**. Dead bodies soon filled the trenches. One soldier said: 'It was like one big grave, only some of us were still alive in it.' By the evening the Australians had captured the ridge. They held it for three days before the Turks fought back and regained some of the ground. The Australians lost 2273 men during the action. New Zealand forces won some territory at nearby Chunuk Bair before they, too, were pushed back by the Turks.

ANZAC troops charging Turkish machine gun positions. The ANZAC troops had a reputation for bravery, daring and courage.

Suvla Bay

Also on 6 August, British troops landed at Suvla Bay. They met with little resistance from the Turks. Once ashore the troops were not sure what to do! Sir Ian Hamilton was at his headquarters aboard a ship anchored off the coast. If he had told the troops to attack the Turks immediately, they could have linked up with the Australians and New Zealanders and gained control of the peninsula. But there was a complete breakdown in communications. Some of the British troops went for a swim while they waited for orders. By the time Hamilton did order an attack, it was too late. The Turks had brought in reinforcements and they were able to hold off the British. Although the British and ANZACs did link up, they were unable to take any more territory.

In October 1915, Hamilton was sacked and replaced as commander by Sir Charles Monro. Two months later the Gallipoli campaign was abandoned.

The Victoria Cross – Britain's highest award for bravery in war. Named after Queen Victoria, it was first awarded during the Crimean War in 1857.

THE VICTORIA CROSS

THE VICTORIA CROSS IS BRITAIN'S HIGHEST AWARD FOR GALLANTRY IN WAR. DURING THE GALLIPOLI CAMPAIGN, TEN ANZAC SOLDIERS WERE AWARDED THE VICTORIA CROSS.

DATE	NAME	COUNTRY	PLACE
20 MAY 1915	ALBERT JACKA	AUSTRALIA	COURTNEY'S POST
7 AUGUST 1915	CYRIL BASSETT	NEW ZEALAND	CHUNUK BAIR
7 AUGUST 1915	LEONARD KEYSOR	AUSTRALIA	LONE PINE
8 AUGUST 1915	WILLIAM SYMONS	AUSTRALIA	LONE PINE
9 AUGUST 1915	ALEXANDER BURTON	AUSTRALIA	LONE PINE
9 AUGUST 1915	WILLIAM DUNSTAN	AUSTRALIA	LONE PINE
9 AUGUST 1915	JOHN HAMILTON	AUSTRALIA	LONE PINE
9 AUGUST 1915	ALFRED SHOUT	AUSTRALIA	LONE PINE
9 AUGUST 1915	FRED TUBB	AUSTRALIA	LONE PINE
30 AUGUST 1915	HUGO THROSSELL	AUSTRALIA	HILL 60

Keith Murdoch

People in Britain, Australia and New Zealand did not know about the bad planning and incompetence of the generals in Gallipoli. The truth was kept from them. The army authorities censored all newspaper articles sent from Gallipoli.

Keith Murdoch, an Australian journalist, went to Gallipoli in the summer of 1915. He was shocked that fighting was still going on. Murdoch believed that the land was so steep it was obvious that the Allies would not be able to win a lot of territory. Hamilton, he said, should have called off the fighting after the landings of 25 April 1915.

Murdoch went to England in September 1915. From here he wrote a long letter to Andrew Fisher, the Australian prime minister. He told the true story of Gallipoli – the pointless fighting, the lack of planning and the disease among the troops. Fisher told the British government, who, in turn, allowed the information to be published in newspapers. This led many people to call for the troops to be withdrawn from Gallipoli.

The Eastern Front 1914–17

The Russians, with an army of five million men, thought they would quickly steamroller the Germans and Austrians to defeat on the **Eastern Front**. But things did not quite turn out as they expected.

The Battle of Tannenberg, 26–30 August 1914

In August 1914, two large Russian armies under General Pavel Rennenkampf and General Alexander Samsonov invaded East Prussia, a part of Germany. The two generals did not like each other, and were not on speaking terms. Hardly a recipe for success! The plan was for the two armies to split to go around the Masurian Lakes. Once past the lakes they would attack the Germans from two sides and move on to Berlin. The Germans, however, picked up the plan on their radios and knew what was happening.

At Tannenberg, Samsonov's army was surrounded by the Germans. Thousands of Russians were driven into swamplands. As they struggled in the water, the Germans machine-gunned them to death. Samsonov was so upset, he shot himself. About 30,000 Russians were killed and a further 100,000 taken prisoner. Between 7 and 14 September, Rennenkampf was beaten in the Battle of the Masurian Lakes, losing a further 100,000 men. The Russians were forced to retreat.

> The Eastern Front involved fighting between Russia and Germany and Austria-Hungary from 1914 to 1917.

The Russians had been beaten because they were poorly organized and were short of weapons and ammunition. The Germans were much better organized and equipped. But the Russian **offensive** had caused the Germans to move thousands of troops from the **Western Front** and this helped the British and French win the Battle of the Marne (see page 7).

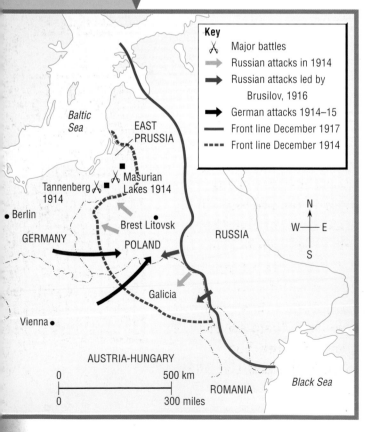

Key
- ✗ Major battles
- → Russian attacks in 1914
- ➡ Russian attacks led by Brusilov, 1916
- ➤ German attacks 1914–15
- —— Front line December 1917
- ----- Front line December 1914

Baltic Sea
EAST PRUSSIA
Tannenberg 1914
Masurian Lakes 1914
Berlin
Brest Litovsk
GERMANY
POLAND
RUSSIA
Galicia
Vienna
AUSTRIA-HUNGARY
ROMANIA
Black Sea

N W E S

0 — 500 km
0 — 300 miles

Slaughter!

This is not war, it is slaughter. Hundreds of thousands of our men are without weapons and have to wait until they can pick up rifles dropped by fallen comrades.

A Russian politician gives his view on the Battle of Tannenberg.

Meanwhile another Russian army won a decisive victory over the Austrians in Galicia. In the Battle of Lemberg (26 August–10 September 1914) the Austrians were forced to retreat over 240 kilometres and suffered 250,000 casualties.

Brusilov strikes back

In the summer of 1915, the Germans and Austrians forced the Russians to retreat further. Thousands of peasants were turned out of their homes and had to flee with the army. The peasants were dressed in summer clothes, and when winter came many froze to death. **Tsar Nicholas II**, fed up with the poor performance of his army generals, made himself commander-in-chief of the Russian army. In February 1916 he ordered a counter-attack against the Germans. It failed and the Russian losses were high. Food was scarce inside Russia and prices shot through the roof. People were growing tired of both the tsar and the war.

In June 1916, General Alexei Brusilov attacked the Austrians near the Romanian border. For a change, his army had plenty of weapons and ammunition. Brusilov gained about 100 kilometres of territory before his troops became exhausted and the advance ground to a halt.

The Russian Revolution: Russia pulls out of the war

The Germans sent reinforcements to the Eastern Front and once again pushed the Russian army back. By now, the Russians were tired and lacking in spirit. They began to desert the army in their thousands. The tsar's popularity was at an all-time low. The people blamed him for the plight of the country and there were strikes and riots in the major cities. In March 1917, the tsar was forced to resign from the throne. In November 1917, the **Bolsheviks** seized power, executed the Tsar and turned Russia into a communist country. The new Bolshevik government, led by Lenin, immediately pulled Russia out of the war and, on 3 March 1918, signed the **Treaty of Brest Litovsk** with Germany. For Russia itself the war had been a disaster, but without the Russian army occupying the Germans in the east the Allies could have lost the war on the Western Front.

Side-show fronts

The side-show fronts were smaller battlegrounds, away from the **Western** and **Eastern Fronts**, in other parts of Europe and around the world.

War in the colonies

Germany lost nearly all its **colonies** to **Allied** forces during the war. In the Pacific the New Zealanders took German Samoa in August 1914, and the Australians captured German New Guinea two weeks later. Japanese troops overran the German trading station at Kiaochow in China, as well as the Marshall, Caroline and Mariana Islands.

In Africa the Allies captured Togoland, German South-west Africa and the Cameroons. Only German East Africa (now Tanzania) remained in German hands. Here General Lettow-Vorbeck managed to beat off the Allied attacks.

The Italian front, 1915–18. Troops on both sides showed great courage fighting in a mountainous area.

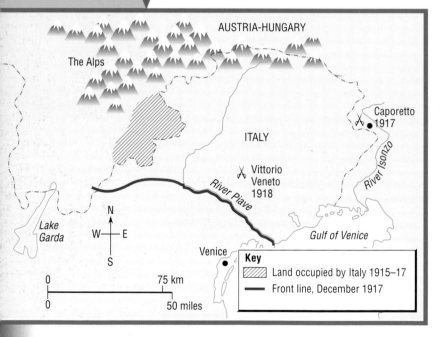

The Italian front

The Italians joined the war on the Allied side in May 1915, hoping to gain land from the Austrians. The two sides fought each other along a front on Italy's north-eastern border with Austria-Hungary. The area is mountainous and fighting was made dangerous by ice, snow blizzards and fog. In November 1917, German troops were sent to help the Austrians. Together they smashed the Italians at the Battle of Caporetto, pushing them back 100 kilometres. The Italians lost at least 250,000 men and a further 400,000 soldiers deserted. The Italian army was near to total collapse. Britain and France sent troops to help. It was not until late 1918 that the Italians were strong enough to mount another attack, when they beat the Austrians at the Battle of Vittorio Veneto.

War in the Middle East

Germany's ally, Turkey, controlled a large amount of land in the Middle East. Britain was worried that the Turks would cut off its oil supplies and block the Suez Canal. Over a million British, Australian, New Zealand

and Indian troops were sent to the area to fight the Turks. In December 1915 the Turks trapped an Allied force inside the town of Kut in Mesopotamia (now Iraq). The town was put under siege and food supplies began to run out. In April 1916 the Allied troops were forced to surrender. Over 12,000 men were captured. Half of them died in prison camps. After this the Allies fought back and took the city of Baghdad in 1917.

Meanwhile a force led by General Edmund Allenby, which had been guarding the Suez Canal, began to advance on Palestine. They pushed the Turks back and captured Jerusalem on 9 December 1917. In September 1918, the Turks were beaten by Allenby at Megiddo. By now the Turks had had enough and pulled out of the war on 31 October.

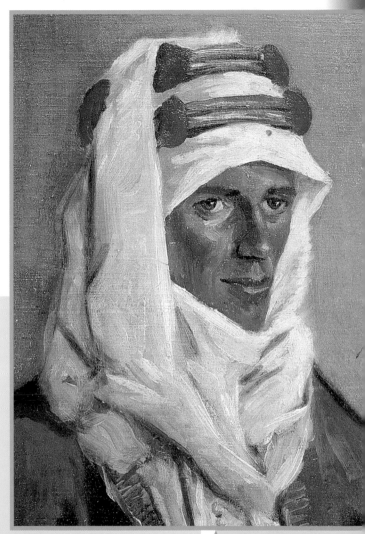

Lawrence of Arabia

Thomas Edward Lawrence, nicknamed 'Ned' by his family, was born in Wales in 1888. He studied History at Oxford University and from 1910 to 1914 worked as an archaeologist in Mesopotamia. It was here that he learned to speak Arabic and got to know the Arab way of life. In 1914 he joined the British army and was sent to serve in Egypt. When the Arabs revolted against their Turkish rulers in 1916, Lawrence was sent to advise them. He quickly won the respect and admiration of the Arab leaders, dressing in Arab clothes and living as one of them. Lawrence led the Arabs in a number of **guerrilla** attacks on the Damascus-Medina railway, the main supply line of the Turkish army. He also captured the port of Akaba from the Turks in 1917, which helped pave the way for Allenby's forces to invade Palestine. The Turks put up a reward of £20,000 for his capture, a huge amount at the time. They actually caught him on one occasion but did not realize who he was! Lawrence of Arabia was killed in a motorbike accident in Dorset, England in 1935.

This painting of Lawrence of Arabia shows how he dressed in Arab clothes. After the war Lawrence worked for the British as an adviser on Arab affairs.

War at sea: the Battle of Jutland 1916

Before the war, both Britain and Germany had built up large navies, which included the new **Dreadnought**-class battleships. But in 1914 the Germans kept their fleet in port, not wanting to risk their expensive ships in a big naval battle.

In August 1914, the Germans had several squadrons of ships in overseas waters. This led to a number of small clashes with **Allied** ships. On 1 November, a German squadron under Admiral von Spee destroyed two British ships at Coronel off the coast of Chile. Revenge for the British came on 8 December, when Admiral Sturdee sank four out of five of von Spee's warships off the Falkland Islands. In the meantime, the Australian cruiser *Sydney* sank the German cruiser *Emden*, which had been attacking Allied shipping in the Indian Ocean. These victories were important. The seas had been cleared of German warships, and troops from the British Empire could sail to Europe without being attacked.

Blockade

The British navy now had control of the sea and it blockaded German ports to stop food supplies reaching Germany. The German High Seas fleet stayed in port. Occasionally, German **battle-cruisers** sailed into the North Sea to bombard towns on the east coast of England, causing civilian casualties. In January 1915, a small naval battle took place on the Dogger Bank, which resulted in the sinking of the *Blucher*, a German battle-cruiser. A major battle, however, was soon to follow.

The Battle of Jutland 1916 was the only major naval battle to take place in World War One.

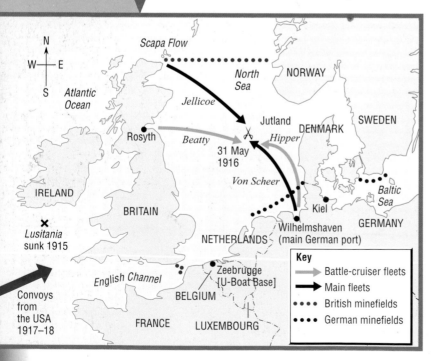

The Battle of Jutland, 31 May 1916

In early 1916 Admiral von Scheer took over command of the German High Seas fleet. He wanted to see some action! On 31 May he ordered a group of battle-cruisers, commanded by Admiral Hipper, to sail into the North Sea. The German plan was to tempt the British Grand Fleet out into open sea and take it by surprise. The British knew what was happening, because they had a copy of the German codebook.

A squadron of British **battle-cruisers**, led by Admiral Beatty, was sent to meet the German ships. The two main fleets of battleships followed behind the battle-cruisers. At 4.00 p.m. the two sets of battle-cruisers met off the coast of Jutland. Within 30 minutes, the British ship *Indefatigable* exploded and sank. Over 1000 sailors went down with it. They were killed outright, drowned or burned to death. Shortly afterwards, the *Queen Mary* also exploded and sank inside 90 seconds, with a loss of 1268 men. A mere eight men were rescued from the water. A shocked Admiral Beatty was heard to say, 'There seems to be something wrong with our bloody ships today!'

BATTLE FACTS – BATTLE OF JUTLAND		
	BRITAIN	GERMANY
NUMBER OF SHIPS	151	103
SHIPS LOST	14	11
MEN KILLED	6100	2550

At 6.00 p.m. the two main fleets joined the battle. More than 250 ships were involved in the exchange of gunfire. Huge Dreadnoughts fired shells each weighing a tonne at each other. Von Scheer realized he was outnumbered and turned for home. The weather was misty, so Admiral Sir John Jellicoe did not give chase. He feared the Germans were luring them towards a pack of **U-boats** and a **minefield**. The battle was over.

Who won?

Both sides claimed a victory. The Germans said they had won because they had sunk more ships and lost fewer men. The British said they were the winners because they still had control of the North Sea and the blockade of Germany was still intact. They were right! The German High Seas fleet stayed in port for the rest of the war.

The Boy Sailor – John Travers Cornwell

Cornwell was 16 years old and a gunner on board the light cruiser, HMS *Chester*, which was hit seventeen times by German shells during the Battle of Jutland. He was badly wounded along with many around him. Despite this he continued to try to fire shells at the German ships. He died from his wounds in Grimsby District Hospital, England on 2 June 1916. He was later awarded the Victoria Cross, which was presented to his mother by King George V.

A painting of John Travers Cornwell during the Battle of Jutland.

War under the sea: the U-boat threat

In 1914 German submarines, known as **U-boats**, sank three British warships in the English Channel. Given a free rein, U-boats were deadly. They would surprise ships by firing torpedoes, or they would surface and fire their guns. The British did not want to risk their warships against the U-boats and always used a screen of **destroyers** to protect them when at sea. Despite this, U-boats might have won the war for Germany.

The U-boat campaign begins

Most of Britain's supplies had to come across the sea either from the USA or the Empire. Germany knew that, if enough food and supply ships going to Britain could be sunk, Britain would be forced to surrender. To begin with the U-boats only attacked ships from countries at war with Germany. Then, on 4 February 1915, the Germans started to attack ships from all countries, whether they were in the war or not. This was called unrestricted submarine warfare.

On 7 May, the British liner *Lusitania* was sunk by a U-boat off the coast of Ireland. The Germans believed (rightly) that it was carrying munitions to Britain, as well as passengers. Among the 1198 people who died were 128 American citizens. The USA was **neutral** at this time and the country was outraged. After this there were fewer U-boat attacks, as the Germans were fearful that the powerful USA might declare war.

A U-boat attacks an Allied ship

After many alterations of course and speed the destroyer passes within 60 yards (60 m) of us. 'Slow ahead!' A look at the torpedo sight on the periscope. Four more degrees until we can fire. 'It's a troopship! Lots of soldiers on board!' whispers the captain. 'Up periscope!' 'No. 1 tube ready!' The periscope rises and the captain looks into it, with his hat pushed back on his head. 'Fire! Dive to 100 feet [30m]! Down periscope!' The torpedo speeds on its way. Twenty seconds later: a hit! The ship is sinking.

Martin Niemoller, a U-boat crew member

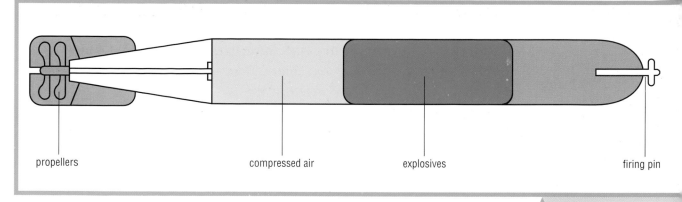

| propellers | compressed air | explosives | firing pin |

Crisis

By 1917 the Germans were anxious to force a victory. They themselves were suffering from food shortages because the British navy had blockaded German ports. On 1 February, they started unrestricted submarine warfare again (a decision that contributed to the USA declaring war on 6 April 1917). By now there were 200 U-boats at sea and they caused havoc with Allied and neutral ships. In April 1917, almost 900,000 tonnes of Allied shipping were sunk. Soon, Britain had just six weeks of food supplies left. It was a crisis. Admiral Jellicoe said, 'It is impossible to go on with the war if losses like this continue.'

Fighting the U-boats

One measure used to fight the U-boat menace was the use of Q-ships. These were merchant ships that had guns hidden on their decks. If a U-boat came to the surface, it was taken by surprise when the Q-ship's guns were uncovered. The Germans, however, grew wise to this tactic and the Q-ships lost their effectiveness.

A World War One torpedo. This deadly weapon had a range of 10,000 metres and was powered by a compressed air engine. It also had a mechanism to control its direction.

The British laid a barrage of 500 mines across the Straits of Dover. This stopped the U-boats from passing down the English Channel and into the Atlantic. Instead, they had to go the long way around the north of Scotland. **Depth charges** were also fired at the U-boats. The best way of countering the U-boats was the convoy system, introduced by David Lloyd George, the British prime minister, in April 1917. Merchant vessels were grouped together and escorted across the sea by destroyers. It proved to be very effective. The number of U-boats destroyed increased and the loss of Allied ships was reduced. This saved Britain from being starved into surrender. But it was a close call.

NUMBERS OF U-BOATS DESTROYED	
1914–16	46
1917	63
1918	69

NUMBER OF ALLIED SHIPS SUNK BY U-BOATS	
1914	3
1915	396
1916	964
1917	2439
1918	1035

War in the air

In 1914 aircraft design was still in its infancy. Aeroplanes were made of wood and canvas and were very flimsy. They were powered by unreliable engines that were liable to cut out in the air. The pilots had to be brave. They took their lives into their hands on every flight! By 1918 aircraft design had made great strides. Although aeroplanes did not have any great effect on the outcome of the war, it was clear that they would change the nature of fighting in the future.

Reconnaissance and observation

No one really knew what part aeroplanes would play in the war. One British general said they were 'useless and an expensive fad'! They were used mainly for reconnaissance flights over enemy lines. An observer sitting behind the pilot made sketches and took photographs of trench systems and troop movements. At sea, aircraft were used to look out for enemy ships and U-boats.

Fighters and air aces

Soon pilots began taking pistols and rifles up with them, hoping to get a pot shot at an enemy plane. Then, in 1915, Anthony Fokker, a Dutch aircraft designer working for the Germans, invented a synchronized gear that enabled a machine gun to fire bullets through the moving propeller blades. This led to the production of fighter planes and to high-speed, one-to-one aerial battles called dogfights. Pilots would move in behind an enemy plane and fire a hail of bullets.

Allied pilots with over five kills were known as 'aces'. Germany did not award its pilots 'ace' status until they had ten kills. 'Aces' were looked upon as heroes, and their adventures were widely reported in newspapers. As the war went on

A painting of a dogfight over the town of Arras in northern France.

LEADING FIGHTER ACES		
NAME	COUNTRY	NUMBER OF KILLS
MANFRED VON RICHTHOFEN ('THE RED BARON')	GERMANY	80
RENÉ FONCK	FRANCE	75
MICK MANNOCK	UK	73
WILLIAM BISHOP	CANADA	72
ROBERT A. LITTLE	AUSTRALIA	47
EDWARD RICKENBACKER	USA	26

fighter aircraft became faster, more reliable and capable of staying in the air for more than two hours. In 1918 the main British fighter, the *Sopwith Camel*, could climb to 5774 metres and had a speed of 185 kph. This was matched by the German *Albatros D–Va* (5700 metres and 187 kph). Both machines were highly manoeuvrable in the hands of a skilful pilot. Aircraft design had come a long way since 1914.

Zeppelins and bombers

The Germans used large airships called Zeppelins to bomb Britain. These ships frightened the British. They always came at night and glided

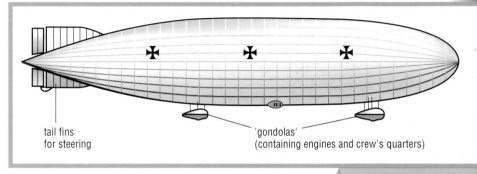

tail fins
for steering

'gondolas'
(containing engines and crew's quarters)

spookily across the sky. Streetlights were turned off and people blacked out their windows so that the Zeppelins could not see their targets. On 19 January 1915 the first Zeppelin raid on Britain took place when two Zeppelins dropped bombs on Yarmouth and King's Lynn, killing four people and injuring sixteen others. At midnight on 31 May 1915, there was a Zeppelin raid on London that killed seven people and caused widespread damage to housing. In 1917 the Germans stopped using Zeppelins and started to use bomber aircraft. The *Gotha IV* bomber raided Britain between 1917 and 1918, causing 850 deaths. In 1918 the British replied with the *Handley Page* bomber. It was capable of attacking Berlin, but the war ended before it was able to do so.

A World War One German Zeppelin. By 1916 the largest Zeppelins were almost 200 metres long, could carry five tons of bombs and had a speed of 40 kph.

Edward Rickenbacker – American 'ace of aces'

Rickenbacker was born in Ohio in 1890. He first made his name as a car racing driver, and in 1911 took part in the very first Indianapolis 500 road race. He was quick to join up when the USA entered the war and was sent to France. Here he worked on the motor-car staff of General Pershing. In March 1918, he was transferred to the Air Service. His quick reflexes made him a brilliant pilot.

Rickenbacker fought 134 dogfights and had 26 kills. On one occasion he fought seven German planes on his own and shot down two of them. In common with other air aces, he had great respect for his enemies. He once said: 'Like all air fighters, I never thought of killing an individual but of shooting down an enemy plane.' Rickenbacker was awarded the Congressional Medal of Honor for his bravery during World War One. He died in 1973.

Enter the USA!

When war broke out in Europe in August 1914, the USA did not take sides. Americans did not want to get involved in a war that was happening 'over there', some 5000 kilometres away. The USA was made up mainly of immigrants from all over Europe, including Britain, Germany and Russia. President Woodrow Wilson said that the USA had to be **neutral**, otherwise its 'mixed population would wage war on each other'. So why did the USA join the war in 1917?

Unrestricted submarine warfare

In May 1915 an angry President Wilson sent several messages of protest to the Germans over the sinking of the *Lusitania* (see page 32). The Germans then agreed not to attack passenger ships without first giving a warning. When unrestricted submarine warfare started again in February 1917, Germany knowingly ran the risk of war with the USA.

A 1917 poster encouraging Americans to join the US army. Germany is depicted as a threat to civilization (Kultur).

The Zimmerman telegram

Arthur Zimmerman was the German Foreign Minister. In January 1917, he sent a telegram to the German ambassador in Mexico, saying he should get the Mexicans to declare war on the USA. British agents found out about the telegram and handed a copy to the USA. It was published in American newspapers on 1 March 1917. The Americans were furious.

The USA declares war

In March 1917, four American ships were sunk by U-boats. This was the final straw for the USA and President Wilson asked **Congress** to declare war on Germany. He said: 'The world must be made safe for democracy. To such a task we can dedicate our lives and our fortunes, everything.' On 6 April, Congress voted by 531 votes to 56 to declare war on Germany. Many Americans were enthusiastic about joining the war and flag-waving crowds paraded down Broadway in New York.

The American Expeditionary Force

In 1917 the USA had an army of just 250,000 men. General John Pershing was put in charge of raising a new army called the American Expeditionary Force (AEF) that would be sent to fight in Europe. It took time to organize and train the AEF, and during 1917 only a small number of Americans reached Europe. But by the end of the war, in November 1918, there were over two million Americans in France, including 400,000 black soldiers.

The arrival of the AEF in Europe raised the morale of the British and French, who were near exhaustion after three years of trench warfare. It was to play an important part in the **Allied** victory on the **Western Front** in 1918.

Soldiers in the AEF were nicknamed 'doughboys'. It is thought the name came from the buttons on the soldiers' uniform, which looked like dumplings made of dough.

General John Joseph Pershing

Born in 1860, Pershing was nicknamed 'Black Jack' because he had commanded a black **cavalry** unit in Cuba in 1898. He suffered a great personal tragedy in 1915, when his wife and three daughters were burned to death in a fire.

Pershing was a stern man who did not suffer fools gladly, and generals who were not doing their jobs were promptly sacked. The Allies wanted the US troops to be under their command. But Pershing refused and insisted that the AEF be kept as a separate force under his control. After the war he was promoted to the rank of General of the American Armies. He died in 1948.

Ludendorff's last throw of the dice

By early 1918 the German people were close to starvation and growing tired of the war. **Erich von Ludendorff**, the German commander, knew that it would not be long before huge numbers of American troops reinforced the **Allies**. He decided to launch a series of all-out attacks on the Allied lines before the Americans arrived. It was Germany's only real chance of winning the war. It was a last throw of the dice.

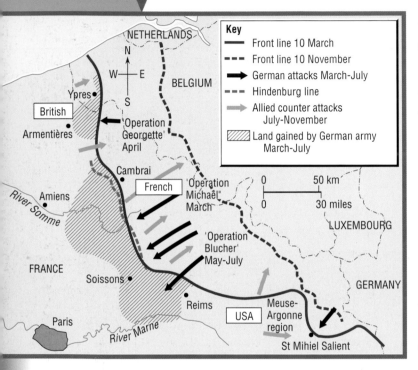

Key
— Front line 10 March
--- Front line 10 November
➡ German attacks March–July
--- Hindenburg line
➡ Allied counter attacks July–November
▨ Land gained by German army March–July

'Operation Michael'

With Russia out of the war, the Germans were able to transfer troops from the **Eastern Front** to the west. During February and March 1918, thousands of trains carried men and equipment into north-eastern France. A huge attack, code-named 'Operation Michael' was to take place against the weakest part of the British lines near the River Somme.

At 4.40 a.m. on 21 March 1918, 7000 guns opened fire on the Allied lines. In five hours, over one million shells were fired, including 250,000 gas shells. The noise was deafening. After this, German stormtroopers – armed with light machine guns, automatic rifles and **flame-throwers** – blazed their way through the Allied lines. In the misty conditions there was chaos and confusion, and the Allies were pushed back. It was like a 'sandcastle before an incoming tide'. It was a war of movement once again. By 5 April the Germans had gained 60 kilometres of territory. But then they were unable to make any further progress.

'Operation Georgette'

On 9 April, Ludendorff attacked the British lines further north near Armentières. 'Operation Georgette' was intended to push the British to the English Channel. For a time it looked like succeeding and a worried General Haig sent a message to the soldiers, in which he said: 'Every position must be held to the last man; there must be no retirement. With our backs to the wall and believing in the justice of our cause, each one of us must fight to the end.' The British put up strong resistance and, by 29 April, they had blocked the Germans advance.

'Operation Blucher'

A third German attack took place between Soissons and Reims on 27 May. The Germans once again broke through and, by July, had reached the River Marne. They were just 70 kilometres away from Paris. A huge gun, nicknamed 'Long Max', was used to bombard Paris, killing 256 civilians. Eventually, the Germans were held up by a combined French–American force and pushed back across the Marne.

German troops climbing over a captured trench as they attack Allied positions north-west of Soissons in June 1918.

The German army had made a great effort, but after three months of fighting the soldiers were exhausted. An outbreak of flu in June did not help matters. The German army had advanced so far into France that it was difficult to keep it supplied. The morale of the troops began to sag and indiscipline crept into the ranks. German soldiers began looting shops, getting drunk and criticizing their officers. By mid-July the tide was turning against them.

A heartfelt letter

Beloved Fritz

Heartiest thanks for your dear letter. If only this cursed war would come to an end. We hope it will soon. Wilhelm Beisz was killed on 1 June. A week ago the Nautmeiers received news that their son Henry had fallen and now they have had a second telegram to say that their youngest son Ludwig has been killed. What a dreadful blow to lose two sons in such a short time.

Fodder is very scarce, so much so that we can hardly feed our cattle. Tomorrow is our sad anniversary. It will be two years since our beloved and only brother was killed, and what a number have fallen in those two years. We ourselves in this small area can count 33, and yet there is no end.

With heartfelt greetings and in the hope of seeing you soon.

Your own dear and faithful
Lena

Extracts from a letter written by Lena Wieden to her soldier husband, Fritz. The letter was dated 16 June 1918. It is thought that the letter was found on his dead body.

The Allies strike back

From 18 July 1918 the Germans were on the back foot. They began to retreat, burning down villages as they did so.

The Battle of Amiens

At 4.20 a.m. on 8 August a combined British, Australian and Canadian force attacked the Germans near Amiens. Over 400 tanks burst through the German lines, supported by bombers and fighter aircraft. The Australians, under the command of **Sir John Monash**, advanced ten kilometres on the first day of fighting. **Erich von Ludendorff** said it was ' the black day of the German army'. By 11 August the **Allies** had captured 4000 guns and taken 30,000 prisoners. The Germans had lost the will to fight and threw down their helmets and rifles almost in relief.

The Manchester Guardian
Tuesday, 23 July 1918

GERMANS TO RETREAT AGAIN BURNING VILLAGES AND STORES

The German retreat from the Marne may extend along a line of 25 miles and to a depth of eight miles or more. The smoke of burning villages and stores has been observed behind the German lines in this region.

With the prisoners taken on Sunday and 45 guns abandoned by the Germans south of the Marne, the Allies have captured about 22,000 prisoners and 460 guns.

These places are on the map on p. 38.

The American front line in the Meuse valley north of Verdun used camouflage left by the Germans who had retreated across the river.

The Meuse-Argonne offensive

On 12 September the American Expeditionary Force under General John Pershing pushed the Germans back in the St Mihiel **salient**, taking 13,000 prisoners. Then, on 26 September, the Americans launched a big attack in the Meuse–Argonne region of eastern France. Slowly but surely they drove the Germans back. Vital railway lines that were used to supply the German army were captured. By November, the Germans had lost all the land they had won earlier in the year. The Americans, however, paid a high price for their victory, with 26,000 dead and 97,000 wounded.

The collapse of Germany

On 29 September Allied forces broke through the **Hindenburg Line**, a heavily fortified German trench system. It was a massive blow. The end of the war was now in sight. By 3 November Germany's allies – Bulgaria, Turkey and Austria – had all surrendered. There was unrest in Germany, with rioting on the streets and a mutiny in the navy. On 9 November 1918 Kaiser Wilhelm II, the emperor of Germany, abdicated and fled to The Netherlands. At 5.00 a.m. on 11 November the Germans signed the **armistice** in a railway carriage at Compiègne, France. All fighting came to an end at eleven o'clock on the same morning. World War One was over.

This cartoon appeared in the Daily Express on 10 November 1918. It shows Kaiser Wilhelm in a Dutch clog. The Allies were unable to arrest him because The Netherlands was a **neutral** country.

The beginning of the end

In early October 1918 **Ludendorff** called a meeting of his General Staff to tell them that Germany had no hope of winning the war. Colonel Albrecht von Thaer later recalled the scene:

Ludendorff stood up, his face was pale and filled with deep worry but his head was still held high. He said it was his duty to tell us that our military condition was terribly serious. The war could no longer be won, but rather a defeat awaited. Soon the enemy, with the help of American troops anxious to fight, would win a victory. Our army would be forced to retreat in disorder across the Rhine. Ludendorff said that he would be asking the Kaiser to seek peace by contacting President Wilson of the USA. As he spoke, quiet sobbing and moaning was audible. Many had tears running down their cheeks.

Victory, but at what price?

News of the **armistice** was greeted with wild enthusiasm. Throughout Britain church bells were rung and people went into the streets waving flags and letting off fireworks. The king and queen were cheered as they drove through London's Hyde Park. In Martin Place, Sydney, huge crowds burned effigies of the Kaiser and sang patriotic songs. There were joyful celebrations across the length and breadth of the USA. Herbert Hamm, of the Student Army Training Corps at the University of Maine, wrote: 'My goodness there was an awful [large] crowd in Bangor.'

Armistice Day in London

November 11: The day has come at last which we have lived for these long four years and three months. The horrible thing is over! Almost all work was stopped and the streets became packed with people. All was one vast pandemonium. Such crowds have never been seen in London. Later, when the King, Queen and Princess Mary (dressed as a VAD) drove down the Mall, the people went wild with delight. Passing the Houses of Parliament on our way home, we saw the great clock once more lit up and heard Big Ben's thundering tones declaring the great fact of peace.

From the diary of Frederick Arthur Robinson, who visited London on Armistice Day

Loss of life

Soon, however, the dreadful cost of the war began to sink in. Over eight million soldiers had lost their lives; more than in any other war to date.

There was talk of a 'lost generation' – men between the ages of 18 and 45 who had died. They certainly included many talented scientists, writers and politicians.

Large monuments to commemorate the dead were built, as communities tried to come to terms with the loss of loved ones.

Material losses

The war left many countries in debt. Britain had spent £9000 million in fighting the war. The government was forced to put up taxes and increase borrowing to pay off its debts. Large areas of France and Belgium had been destroyed by shellfire. Forests and woodland had been obliterated. Towns such as Ypres in Belgium had to be completely rebuilt.

How the Daily Mirror reported the celebrations in London on Armistice Day 1918.

Itchen Abbas, Hampshire

A memorial cross has been erected in the churchyard in memory of all those from this village who have made 'the great sacrifice'. The cross which is of Swanage cliff stone [from Dorset] stands 15 feet [5m] high and is placed close to the churchyard gate so that all who pass by may see it. It will be a very striking memorial of the Great War.

From a report in the *Hampshire Chronicle*, 1919. Itchen Abbas is a small Hampshire village. Ten men from the village lost their lives in the war.

Never again!

People said that such a war should never be allowed to happen again. On 11 November 1918, David Lloyd George, the British prime minister, told the House of Commons, 'I hope we may say that, thus, this fateful morning, came an end to all wars.' His sentiments turned out to be wishful thinking. Under the 1919 Treaty of Versailles, the Allied powers made Germany pay a heavy price for its part in the war. Large amounts of territory were taken from Germany and it was ordered to pay £6600 million in war damages. The terms of the treaty were dictated to the Germans. They were not allowed to negotiate any part of the treaty. Many Germans felt humiliated and there was a huge amount of resentment. This was one of the major reasons why, in 1939, the world was at war once again.

This huge monument is at Thiepval, near the town of Albert, on the River Somme in France. It lists the names of 73,412 soldiers who died in the Battle of the Somme and whose bodies were never found.

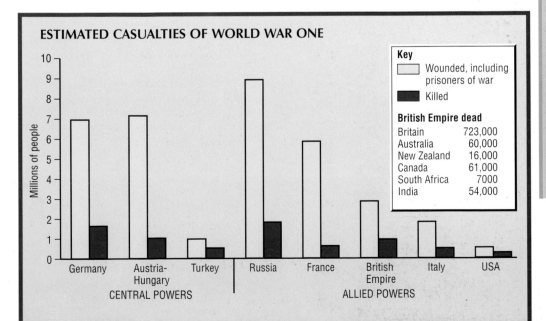

ESTIMATED CASUALTIES OF WORLD WAR ONE

Millions of people (y-axis, 0–10)

Central Powers: Germany, Austria-Hungary, Turkey
Allied Powers: Russia, France, British Empire, Italy, USA

Key
- Wounded, including prisoners of war
- Killed

British Empire dead

Britain	723,000
Australia	60,000
New Zealand	16,000
Canada	61,000
South Africa	7000
India	54,000

World War One timeline

	WESTERN FRONT	EASTERN FRONT	GALLIPOLI/ MIDDLE EAST	ITALIAN FRONT AND SIDE-SHOW FRONTS	AIR AND SEA
1914	28 June: assassination of Archduke Franz Ferdinand 5–9 Sept: Battle of the Marne End of 1914: Trenches dug from English Channel to Swiss border	26–30 Aug: Battle of Tannenberg 7–14 Sept: Battle of the Masurian Lakes	Oct: Turkey enters war on the side of Germany	German colonies in Africa and Pacific Ocean captured by Allies	Nov: German ships sink 2 British ships at Coronel *Emden* sunk by HMAS *Sydney* Dec: British sink German warships off the Falkland Islands
1915	April: Gas used for the first time by German army Sept: British use gas in the Battle of Loos		25 April: First landings on Gallipoli peninsula 6 Aug: Landings at Suvla Bay Dec: Kut besieged by Turks Evacuation of troops from Gallipoli	May: Italy enters war on side of Allies	Jan: *Blucher* sunk by British on the Dogger Bank First Zeppelin raid on Britain Feb: First unrestricted submarine warfare campaign May: *Lusitania* sunk
1916	Feb: Start of the Battle of Verdun 1 July–18 Nov: Battle of the Somme 15 Sept: Tanks used for first time	June: Russian counter-attack under Brusilov	April: Surrender of Kut to Turks T. E. Lawrence organizes guerrilla attacks on Turks		31 May: Battle of Jutland Zeppelin raid on London
1917	April: USA enters war 7 June: Allies capture Messines Ridge 31 July–10 Nov: Third Battle of Ypres 6 Nov: Capture of Passchendaele 20 Nov: Battle of Cambrai	March: Tsar Nicholas II abdicates Nov: Bolsheviks seize control of Russia Dec: Russia withdraws from the war	Dec: Capture of Jerusalem by Allenby	Oct/Nov: Battle of Caporetto	1 Feb: Germany restarts unrestricted submarine warfare April: Convoy system started Germans start using bombers to raid Britain
1918	21 March: Operation Michael 8 August: Battle of Amiens Sept: Meuse-Argonne offensive 11 Nov: Armistice signed	3 March: Treaty of Brest Litovsk between Germany and Russia 3 Nov: Austria surrenders	31 Oct: Turkey withdraws from the war	Sept: Bulgaria withdraws from the war Oct/Nov: Battle of Vittorio Veneto	

Map of the world at war

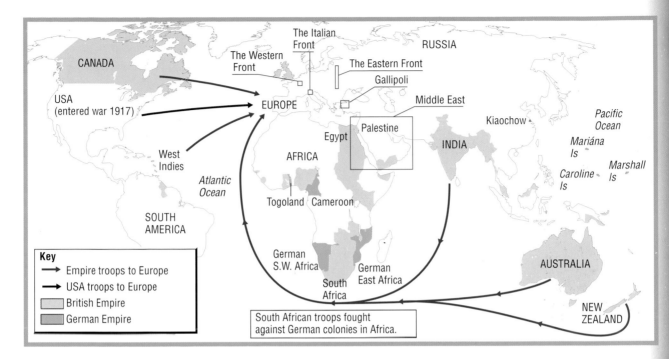

Key
→ Empire troops to Europe
→ USA troops to Europe
■ British Empire
■ German Empire

South African troops fought against German colonies in Africa.

Further reading and places of interest

Further reading

Books

The Great War 1914–18, Peter Fisher, Collins Educational, 1993

The First World War, Nigel Kelly, Heinemann, 1989

The Western Front, Rosemary Rees, Heinemann, 1995

Britain and the Great War, John Robottom, Longman, 1996

Fighting in World War I, Stephen Hoare, Batsford, 1986

The First World War, ed. Stewart Ross, Wayland, 1989

War Horse, Michael Morpurgo, Puffin, 1989

Sources

Chronicles of The Great War: the Western Front 1914–18, Peter Simkins, Colour Library Direct, 1997

The World War One Source Book, Philip J. Haythornthwaite, Arms and Armour Press, 1992

Tommy Goes to War, Malcolm Brown, Dent and Sons, 1978

Voices and Images of the Great War, Lynn Macdonald, Penguin Books, 1991

World War One websites

World War One:
www.bbc.co.uk/history/wwone.shtml

First World War Encyclopaedia:
www.spartacus.schoolnet.co.uk/FWW.htm

Hellfire Corner: www.fylde.demon.co.uk

The Imperial War Museum, London:
www.iwm.org.uk/

The Doughboy Center:
www.worldwar1.com/dbc/ghq1arm.htm

CD-Rom

World War 1, Flagtower, 1995

Places of interest

Imperial War Museum
Lambeth Road
London
SE1 6HZ
Tel: 020 7416 5320
email: mail@iwm.org.uk

Glossary

alliance a union of countries who join together for a common purpose; for example, defending themselves against a common enemy

Allies global term for countries united against Germany and Austria-Hungary

ANZAC short for 'Australian and New Zealand Army Corps'

armistice a cease-fire which precedes the making of a peace treaty

Balkans the south-eastern part of Europe

battle-cruiser a heavy gunned ship, smaller and faster than a battleship but made of lighter armour

bayonet a long blade for stabbing, fixed to a rifle muzzle

Bolsheviks a political party in Russia that believed in communism. The Bolsheviks, led by Lenin, seized power in Russia during the Russian Revolution in November 1917

Brest Litovsk, Treaty of signed on 3 March 1918 between Germany and Russia. Russia was made to pay war damages to the Germans and to give up land in Poland and the Ukraine

casualty clearing station a hospital behind the front line where wounded soldiers were taken for surgery

cavalry soldiers on horseback

colonies countries that were taken over and run by another country

Congress the 'parliament' of the USA made up of the Senate and the House of Representatives

depth charge a bomb which explodes under the water

destroyer a small, fast warship

Dreadnought a super battleship first built in Britain in 1906 and copied by other navies

Eastern Front an important area of fighting in eastern Germany, Poland and Galicia

empire a large group of countries under the control of another country. The British Empire included Australia, New Zealand, South Africa, Canada, India and the West Indies.

fascine a large bundle of sticks which was dropped into a trench, enabling the tank to cross it

flame-thrower a weapon, fuelled by gas or paraffin, which shoots out a large flame

great powers the most powerful countries in Europe in 1914 (Britain, Germany, France, Russia, Italy and Austria-Hungary)

grenades a small bomb which is thrown at an enemy

guerrilla a soldier who mounts surprise hit-and-run attacks on a larger enemy. Guerrilla soldiers usually operate in small groups.

Hindenburg Line a defensive German trench system that ran from Arras to Laon in north-eastern France. It was made up of deep trenches and concrete shelters that were protected by thick barbed wire.

industrialized when a country's economy is based on factories that produce large amounts of goods and where most people live in towns and cities

infantry soldiers on foot

latrines lavatories in the trenches, usually a hole in the ground containing a bucket or large biscuit tin which was emptied at night

minefields on land areas where explosive devices were planted in the ground. At sea minefields were areas where spherical objects made of iron and full of explosives were floated beneath the surface. They were detonated when the hull of a ship hit them.

neutral not taking sides in a war

No Man's Land the area between the two opposing lines of trenches during World War One

offensive a large, planned attack on the enemy

pals battalion a volunteer group of men from the same town or locality

pillboxes small concrete fortifications

salient a bulge jutting into a line of defence or attack

U-boat a German submarine, short for *Unterseeboot*

Western Front an important area of fighting during World War One, made up of two parallel lines of trenches (one German) and one Allied). The trenches stretched for 650 kilometres from the English Channel to the Swiss border.

Some famous people

Birdwood, Sir William British-born general who was appointed to command the ANZAC forces in 1914. He was popular with the troops, who nicknamed him 'Birdy'

Haig, Sir Douglas was in command at the Battle of the Somme (1916) and the third battle of Ypres (1917). He was heavily criticised for the terrible British losses.

Kitchener, Lord British Secretary of State for War in 1914. He was responsible for raising volunteers to fight in World War One.

Ludendorff, Erich von German general who planned the attack on Verdun in 1916 and the final German Spring offensive on the Allies in 1918

Monash, Sir John Australian lieutenant-general who took over from Birdwood as commander of the Australian Corps in 1918

Tsar Nicholas II Emperor of Russia, who was forced to give up the throne in March 1917

Index